SOVIET HUMOR
The Best of KROKODIL

By
The Editors of
KROKODIL
Magazine

Andrews and McMeel   A Universal Press Syndicate Company   Kansas City • New York

Published under license from VNESHTORGIZDAT, U.S.S.R.

Published in association with Educational Services Corporation.

ISBN: 0-8362-1834-5

Library of Congress Catalog Card Number: 88-83866

Cartoons and KROKODIL Editor's Foreword translated from the Russian by Gerald Mikkelson and Margaret Winchell.

Cover cartoons by **S. Tiunin**
С. ТЮНИН

LET'S LAUGH TOGETHER!

A few words to our American readers
from
Aleksey Pyanov, Editor-in-Chief of the magazine *Krokodil*

Just five years ago even the most inveterate optimist wouldn't have risked making such a suggestion. And had he dared to do so, he would certainly have provoked ironic smiles from both sides, for Soviet-American relations at that time left no room for laughter. The road between us was all too cluttered with obstacles to mutual understanding and trust.

We are now slowly but surely dismantling the barriers of outmoded stereotypes as we clear a path toward cooperation and a firm and lasting peace—toward a nuclear-free world. This is a difficult task, but a noble and essential one. And it will be much easier to accomplish if we work at it with smiles on our faces and a good joke now and then.

The leaders of our two nations set an inspiring example when they opened a dialogue based on a new way of thinking, on a search for new approaches to the resolution of the most pressing problems of our time. These contacts gave birth to the initiative that led to the first exchange of Soviet and American humorists in the whole history of relations between our countries. The idea was first put forth by our American colleagues Herbert Cummings, president of the Workshop Library on World Humor, and Dr. James Boren, president of the International Association of Professional Bureaucrats. Two years ago they were the first to say, "Come visit us in America! And bring along lots of smiles, funny stories, and humorous cartoons!"

And so we came. A delegation from the magazine *Krokodil* arrived armed with everything necessary for a two-week journey around the United States. But the demand for Soviet humor turned out to be so great that, as the saying goes, we had to replenish our stocks along the way—in Washington, Tempe, Los Angeles, Philadelphia, Nashville. . . .

Our trip was not only enjoyable but also instructive. It convinced us that we can indeed laugh together: at ourselves, at each other, and at our recent fears.

"Exploding laughter rather than exploding bombs!" This was the slogan Jim Boren suggested for the exchange of humorists. And it was enthusiastically accepted by both sides of "the summit meeting of humorists."

Among those laughing were students and housewives, senators and policemen, reporters and businessmen, scholars and artists. And this laughter was our greatest and most welcome reward. It generously repaid us for striving to destroy the myth that Soviet people are gloomy, withdrawn, and stern.

The words heard most often at the meetings and symposia, the press conferences and debates in the U.S. were perestroika and glasnost. We saw that for Americans these words were taking on real meaning.

And then, one year later, American humorists came to the U.S.S.R. The same irrepressible Jim Boren led their delegation. He was accompanied, as he had been in the U.S., by his wife Alice and also by the satirical writer Art Buchwald, who is well known in our country, by cartoonist Jim Berry, and by art historian Dr. Ronald Paulson. This high-spirited team visited Moscow, Leningrad, Tallinn, Kiev, and even Chernobyl. During dozens of public meetings they engaged in pointed discussions, heated arguments, and professional dialogues, seasoned, as they had been in the U.S., with genuine laughter. Laughter followed Boren's jokes and Buchwald's remarkable tales, Berry's cartoons, and Paulson's astute commentaries.

For the most part, the first exchange of humorists was a success. The Americans even called it a historic event. This might be an overstatement, but let's not be stingy with the plaudits—let's do them justice! Especially since our contacts are continuing to develop. One example is the collection of cartoons you now hold in your hands. This book is the brainchild of that very exchange, which brought Donna Martin, editorial director of Andrews and McMeel, to Moscow. While we were drinking tea in the traditional Russian manner, the idea of a U.S. edition of selected *Krokodil* cartoons took shape.

Since this book is the first of its kind, I would like to say a few words about the magazine that is its main source.

Krokodil, with a circulation of 5,000,300, is the oldest satirical magazine in our country. It began publication sixty-seven years ago. We are proud that Vladimir Ilich Lenin was one of its founders. He highly valued the power of satire and often used classical images from Russian satirical literature in his own writings.

Almost all our leading writers and artists have contributed to *Krokodil.* And this tradition continues today. Our nation, which is now undergoing a revolutionary restructuring of society, sees its practical daily problems reflected on the pages of the magazine. Our readers assist us in this effort—they send us about one hundred thousand letters each year.

Since this collection is limited to cartoons from recent years, it does not portray the magazine's entire history. But, as the Russian saying goes, "The first step is always the hardest." We hope that our cooperation will continue and that American readers will become familiar not only with the cartoons but also with the short stories, novellas, poetry, and humorous ditties of Soviet writers. Then Americans will have a better knowledge of our country and our people, for it is well known that the soul of a people resides in its humor. And *Krokodil* is already preparing to publish a book of satire from the U.S.

So, what do you say! Let's laugh together!

FOREWORD

That anyone could compile an anthology of Soviet cartoons will surprise many Americans. In the United States, the U.S.S.R. is usually depicted as either a bleak, gray land where dumpy peasant women sweep the sidewalks or a sinister conspiracy of a country, bristling with missiles, spies, and aging generals in medal-encrusted uniforms. In both scenarios, the graphic arts are restricted to garish, "heroic" murals on the walls of tractor factories.

These stereotypes don't allow for the existence of much laughter, let alone a humor magazine that publishes 5.3 million copies every ten days. (*Time* prints approximately 4.7 million copies each week; *Newsweek*, 3.3 millon.) Apparently a lot of Soviet citizens are neither sweeping the sidewalks nor spying on the West, but living ordinary, middle-class lives and laughing at the world around them.

Although laughter is often cited as one of the few truly universal human experiences, the humor in many cartoons is predicated on the shared experiences of a specific social, cultural, or ethnic group. These drawings from *Krokodil* reveal that many situations we regard as uniquely American are actually the product of daily life in any industrialized urban society.

E. Shukaev's cartoon of a pair of effete yuppies who've been so busy overfurnishing their home that they "never found time to have kids" (page 19) seems so American that it could have appeared in the *New Yorker*; his drawing of a pair of lovers sending Cupid out for vodka (page 44) might have been in *Playboy*. The little boy in V. Spel'nikov's cartoon who plans to make his parents play the violin and take cod liver oil when he grows up (page 113) sounds like Calvin in Bill Watterson's Calvin and Hobbes.

Although the *Krokodil* artists use some familiar situations (cartoon wives with rolling pins awaiting errant husbands), they tend to employ more literary references than American cartoonists. To understand E. Milutka's drawing of a hang gliding fox (page 103), the reader must know La Fontaine's fable about the Fox and the Crow—a story familiar to European schoolchildren, but less widely known in the U.S. Don Quixote is depicted as the comic figure Cervantes envisioned, rather than the poetic dreamer of *Man of La Mancha*.

The drawings themselves tend to be as simple as many contemporary American comic strips and magazine panels, and often suggest the influence of Western humorists. The rough lines in the cartoon of two shivering swimmers by L. Soifertis (page 80) recalls the looser style Helen Hokinson used in some of her captionless *New Yorker* drawings. I. Novikov's scruffy chef who cooks by feel (page 123) looks like one of Jim Unger's Herman characters, while V. Shkarban's "Orpheus in Hades" (page 78) is reminiscent of Emett's postwar work in *Punch*.

Other drawings reflect regional graphic traditions: Characters similar to the little man with the cucumber nose in V. Peskov's cartoon (page 173) appear in many Eastern European animated films, including Jedan Zivota's *One Day of Life* (Yugoslavia) and Feodor Khitruk's *The Island* (U.S.S.R.). Aside from the carrot nose, the charming snow woman walking her snow dog in R. Drukman's drawing (page 127) doesn't look anything like the familiar Frosty.

Although the work of certain artists stands out, most of the cartoons from *Krokodil* display a curious stylistic uniformity: Nearly everyone draws simple, outline figures. The reader looks in vain for the bold individuality of the great American cartoonists: Charles Addams's delicately macabre ink washes, Edward Koren's fuzzy clusters of broken lines, James Thurber's meandering outlines, Peter Arno's virtuoso brushwork.

The draftsmanship is more polished in the captionless works that focus on social problems, notably alcoholism and drug abuse. These often powerful drawings suggest editorial illustrations, rather than humorous cartoons. It's easy to imagine S. Tiunin's picture of a drug addict literally blowing his mind (page 146) or A. Pshenianikov's poignant drawing of a child walking with the shadow of his alcoholic father (page 143) appearing on the Op-Ed page of the Sunday *New York Times*. The grim, robotic head sprouting carnations (page 149) by G. Basyrov is as striking as any image of perestroika that has appeared in the West.

But the most interesting cartoons for Western audiences are the ones that criticize the Soviet government and/or bureaucracy. Their very existence is a surprise: American readers assume that satirical drawings like E. Vedernikov's bored executive who gets in trouble for making nonstandard doodles on a scratch pad (page 166) or S. Tiunin's mobile of a lone, sweating worker supporting a group of idle functionaries (page 152) would earn the artists one-way tickets to Siberia.

These cartoons suggest that the frustrations of daily life in the U.S.S.R. parallel those in the United States. Civil servants are apparently as uncivil in Tallinn as they are in Los Angeles; bureaucracies are as unresponsive to human needs by the Volga as they are by the Potomac. Anyone who has tried to pursue a problem through the labyrinth of the federal government can appreciate I. Smirnov's portrait of a faceless official whose desk dams a river, turning a valley into a desert (page 155). Office workers everywhere will immediately understand V. Mokhov's drawing, "Staff reduction" (page 163): The bureaucratic basilisk will regrow its tail with depressing speed.

At a time when many Americans are reevaluating their impressions of the U.S.S.R., the glimpses of Soviet daily life in these cartoons—and the shared laughter they engender—may foster an understanding between our countries that transcends politicians' statements about glasnost.

—CHARLES SOLOMON, critic and historian of animation and cartooning

Part 1
RELATIONSHIPS

V. Shkarban
В. ШКАРБАН

E. Milutka
Е. МИЛУТКА

N. Vorontsov
Н. ВОРОНЦОВ

I. Novikov
И. НОВИКОВ

"Children? They're out of style now."

—ДЕТИ? ЭТО СЕЙЧАС НЕМОДНО.

E. Shukaev

Е. ШУКАЕВ

A. Pomazkov
А. ПОМАЗКОВ

G. Karavaeva

Г. КАРАВАЕВА

V. Vladov
В. ВЛАДОВ

14

"Now I'll have to get a new husband. This one doesn't go with the decor."

—ОСТАЛОСЬ ТОЛЬКО МУЖА ЗАМЕНИТЬ, ОН НЕ СООТВЕТСТВУЕТ МОЕМУ ИНТЕРЬЕРУ.

L. Filippova
Л. ФИЛИППОВА

A. Pomazkov
А. ПОМАЗКОВ

16

"I used to work in a meat-packing plant."

—ОДНО ВРЕМЯ Я РАБОТАЛ НА МЯСОКОМБИНАТЕ.

E. Milutka
Е. МИЛУТКА

E. Milutka
Е. МИЛУТКА

18

"Quite a nest we've got for ourselves. It's just too bad we never found time to have kids."

—СЛАВНОЕ У НАС ГНЕЗДЫШКО ПОЛУЧИЛОСЬ. ЖАЛЬ ТОЛЬКО, ЧТО ДЕТИШЕК ЗАВЕСТИ НЕДОСУГ БЫЛО.

E. Shukaev

Е. ШУКАЕВ

"Would you like to go for a stroll?"

—ПОЙДЕМТЕ ПРОГУЛЯЕМСЯ?

V. Uborevich-Borovskii
В. УБОРЕВИЧ-БОРОВСКИЙ

20

"Don't be afraid, little one. That's just Daddy who's come to say goodnight."

—НЕ ПУГАЙСЯ, ДЕТОЧКА. ЭТО ЖЕ ТВОЙ ПАПА ПРИШЕЛ ПОЖЕЛАТЬ ТЕБЕ СПОКОЙНОЙ НОЧИ.

G. Andrianov
Г. АНДРИАНОВ

A. Umiarov
А. УМЯРОВ

22

"Relax, it's not the police. It's just burglars."

—УСПОКОЙСЯ, ЭТО НЕ МИЛИЦИЯ, ЭТО ВОРЫ.

S. Bogachev
С. БОГАЧЕВ

"Now the old folks do aerobics every Saturday—so we have to babysit their grandchildren . . ."

—ТЕПЕРЬ КАЖДУЮ СУББОТУ У ПРЕДКОВ ЗАНЯТИЯ ПО АЭРОБИКЕ—ВОТ И ПРИХОДИТСЯ СИДЕТЬ С ИХ ВНУКАМИ . . .

A. Eliseev

А. ЕЛИСЕЕВ

24

"I think the Sidorovs have gone overboard in their infatuation with antiques."

—ПО-МОЕМУ, СИДОРОВЫ УЖ СЛИШКОМ УВЛЕКЛИСЬ СТАРИНОЙ.

G. Andrianov
Г. АНДРИАНОВ

25

"We're so lucky that the computer helped us find each other."

—КАКОЕ СЧАСТЬЕ, ЧТО КОМПЬЮТЕР ПОМОГ НАМ НАЙТИ ДРУГ ДРУГА!

N. Lisogorskii
Н. ЛИСОГОРСКИЙ

"Why don't you ever bill and coo anymore, my dear?"
"Why should I? We're already married."

—ЧТО НЕ ПОЕШЬ БОЛЬШЕ, ДОРОГОЙ?
—А ЗАЧЕМ? ВЕДЬ МЫ УЖЕ ЖЕНАТЫ.

A. Eliseev

А. ЕЛИСЕЕВ

V. Spel'nikov
В. СПЕЛЬНИКОВ

28

"God! He doesn't even know how to live right, and he still lives to be a hundred . . ."

—ЭХ! И ЖИТЬ-ТО ПО-ЧЕЛОВЕЧЕСКИ НЕ УМЕЕТ, А ВЕДЬ СТО ЛЕТ ЖИВЕТ . . .

M. Skobelev
М. СКОБЕЛЕВ

A. Aleshichev

А. АЛЕШИЧЕВ

"Promise me, dearest, that you'll carry me in your arms even after the builders are finished."

—ОБЕЩАЙ, ДОРОГОЙ, ЧТО БУДЕШЬ НОСИТЬ МЕНЯ НА РУКАХ И ПОСЛЕ БЛАГОУСТРОЙСТВА МИКРОРАЙОНА.

Iu. Cherepanov
Ю. ЧЕРЕПАНОВ

Elle Tikerpiae
ЭЛЛЕ ТИКЕРПЯЭ

A. Aleshichev
А. АЛЕШИЧЕВ

An inhabited island.

ОБИТАЕМЫЙ ОСТРОВ

V. Uborevich-Borovskii
В. УБОРЕВИЧ-БОРОВСКИЙ

E. Osipov
Е. ОСИПОВ

"Oh, my savior, I would marry you, but your salary is awfully small . . ."

—О МОЙ СПАСИТЕЛЬ, Я БЫ ВЫШЛА ЗА ВАС ЗАМУЖ, НО ОКЛАД У ВАС ОЧЕНЬ
МАЛЕНЬКИЙ . . .

G. Karavaeva
Г. КАРАВАЕВА

36

N. Belevtsev
Н. БЕЛЕВЦЕВ

The modern serenade.

СОВРЕМЕННАЯ СЕРЕНАДА.

B. Vorob'ev

Б. ВОРОБЬЕВ

"240 rubles a month, a big apartment, one child from my first marriage, no car or summer cottage . . ."

—ОКЛАД ДВЕСТИ СОРОК, КВАРТИРА ДВУХКОМНАТНАЯ, РЕБЕНОК ОТ ПЕРВОГО БРАКА, МАШИНЫ И ДАЧИ НЕТ . . .

N. Belevtsev
Н. БЕЛЕВЦЕВ

"And now, Vera, move the red king to QB5."

—ТЕПЕРЬ, ВЕРА, ПЕРЕДВИНЬ КОРОЛЯ С А7 НА В6.

41

E. Shabel'nik
Е. ШАБЕЛЬНИК

"Did you take any bribes?"
"Yes."
"Then go wash your hands."

—ВЗЯТКИ БРАЛ?
—БРАЛ.
—ИДИ МОЙ РУКИ.

V. Chizhikov
В. ЧИЖИКОВ

42

"Whadaya mean, are we serious? Would I be carrying him here in my arms if it weren't true love?"

—КАК ЭТО ТАК—ФИКТИВНЫЙ? СТАЛА БЫ Я ТАСКАТЬ ЕГО НА РУКАХ, ЕСЛИ БЫ НЕ ЛЮБИЛА.

I. Novikov
И. НОВИКОВ

"Here, kid, go get us a bottle of vodka."

—ПАЦАН, СЛЕТАЙ ЗА БУТЫЛКОЙ.

E. Shukaev
Е. ШУКАЕВ

44

Part 2
LIFESTYLE

V. Soldatov
В. СОЛДАТОВ

S. Spasskii
С. СПАССКИЙ

46

V. Vladov
В. ВЛАДОВ

A. Aleshichev
А. АЛЕШИЧЕВ

V. Vladov
В. ВЛАДОВ

"How many times have I sworn not to sleep on the job!"

—СКОЛЬКО РАЗ ДАВАЛ СЕБЕ ЗАРОК НЕ СПАТЬ ДНЕМ НА РАБОТЕ!

M. Skobelev
М. СКОБЕЛЕВ

V. Mileiko
В. МИЛЕЙКО

O. Tesler
О. ТЕСЛЕР

A. Umiarov
А. УМЯРОВ

54

O. Tesler
О. ТЕСЛЕР

V. Vladov

В. ВЛАДОВ

O. Tesler
О. ТЕСЛЕР

L. Nasyrov
Л. НАСЫРОВ

58

A. Umiarov

А. УМЯРОВ

M. Valiakhmetov

М. ВАЛИАХМЕТОВ

V. Dubov
В. ДУБОВ

E. Gavrilin
Е. ГАВРИЛИН

E. Osipov
Е. ОСИПОВ

"Today, class, we're going to make computers out of modeling clay!"

O. Tesler
О. ТЕСЛЕР

A. Aleshichev
А. АЛЕШИЧЕВ

Critical remarks.

A. Krylov
А. КРЫЛОВ

L. Nasyrov
Л. НАСЫРОВ

68

A. Bavykin
А. БАВЫКИН

A. Aleshichev
А. АЛЕШИЧЕВ

70

"There's a rumor going around that there's a lot of feed down south . . ."

G. Ogorodnikov
Г. ОГОРОДНИКОВ

"From now on he'll know what kind of haircut you get for forty kopecks and no tip!"

—НАПЕРЕД БУДЕТ ЗНАТЬ, КАК СТРИЧЬСЯ ЗА СОРОК КОПЕЕК!

V. Polukhin
В. ПОЛУХИН

M. Vaisbord
М. ВАЙСБОРД

"Who is that a statue of?"
"Our warehouse manager. He made it out of materials he salvaged while building his summer cottage."

—КОМУ ЭТОТ ПАМЯТНИК?
—НАШЕМУ ЗАВСКЛАДОМ. ОН ВОЗДВИГ ЕГО ИЗ МАТЕРИАЛОВ, КОТОРЫЕ СЭКОНОМИЛ НА СТРОИТЕЛЬСТВЕ ДАЧИ.

V. Skrylev
В. СКРЫЛЕВ

V. Burkin
В. БУРКИН

I. Novikov

И. НОВИКОВ

76

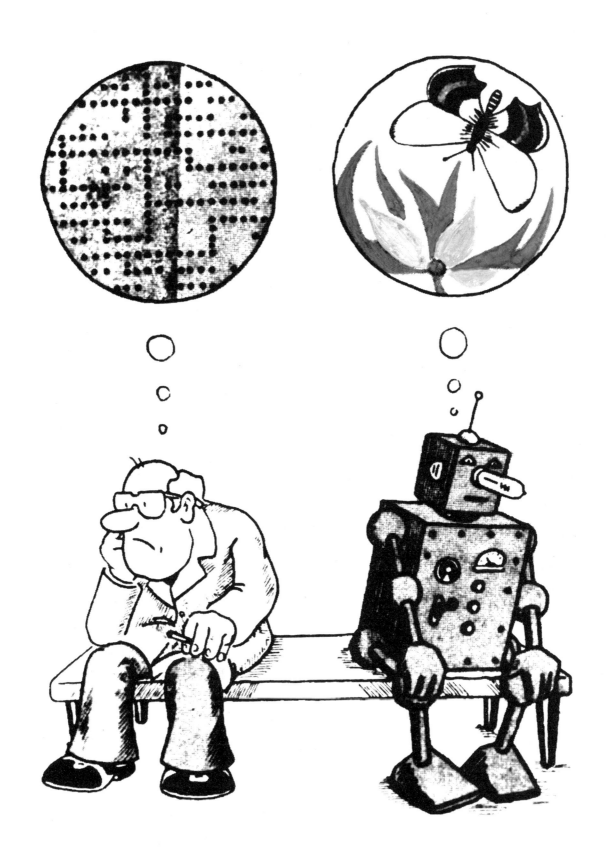

V. **Ashmanov**
В. АШМАНОВ

Orpheus in Hades.

ОРФЕЙ В АДУ.

V. Shkarban
В. ШКАРБАН

A. Aleshichev
А. АЛЕШИЧЕВ

"But it's still warmer here than at home. My wife writes that they've turned off the central heating."

—А ВСЕ-ТАКИ ЗДЕСЬ ТЕПЛЕЙ, ЧЕМ ДОМА. ЖЕНА ПИШЕТ, ЧТО ОТОПЛЕНИЕ ВЫКЛЮЧИЛИ.

L. Soifertis
Л. СОЙФЕРТИС

V. Iakovlev
В. ЯКОВЛЕВ

"What a powerful guy this Sidorov is, a regular Julius Caesar!"

—НУ И СИЛЕН ЭТОТ СИДОРОВ, ПРЯМО ЧТО ТВОЙ ЮЛИЙ ЦЕЗАРЬ!

O. Tesler
О. ТЕСЛЕР

"We've been instructed to get closer to our youngsters!"

E. Osipov
Е. ОСИПОВ

"We'll never outscreech them. Let's find a different roof!"

—НАМ ИХ НЕ ПЕРЕКРИЧАТЬ, ПОЙДЕМ НА ДРУГУЮ КРЫШУ!

G. Andrianov

Г. АНДРИАНОВ

"Palm this off on somebody—I'm afraid to taste it."

—ПОДСУНЬ-КА КОМУ-НИБУДЬ, А ТО Я ПРОБУ БОЮСЬ ПРИНИМАТЬ.

E. Shcheglov
Е. ЩЕГЛОВ

"Why are you three bars ahead of the orchestra?"
"I would like to leave work early today."

—ЧЕГО ВЫ МЧИТЕСЬ НА ТРИ ТАКТА ВПЕРЕДИ ОРКЕСТРА?
—Я ХОТЕЛ БЫ ОТПРОСИТЬСЯ СЕГОДНЯ С РАБОТЫ ПОРАНЬШЕ.

87

M. Skobelev
М. СКОБЕЛЕВ

B. Erenburg
Б. ЭРЕНБУРГ

"Son, I've been wanting to have a serious talk with you for a long time . . ."

—ДАВНО Я ХОТЕЛ С ТОБОЙ СЕРЬЕЗНО ПОГОВОРИТЬ, СЫНОК . . .

E. Shukaev
Е. ШУКАЕВ

"This play is the work of an innovative director . . ."

—ЭТОТ СПЕКТАКЛЬ НАМ ПОСТАВИЛ ОДИН РЕЖИССЕРНОВАТОР . . .

Iu. Andreev
Ю. АНДРЕЕВ

"You call this a museum? Why, you should see my house!"

—И ЭТО МУЗЕЙ? ДА ВЫ У МЕНЯ ДОМА БЫЛИ!

L. Samoilov
Л. САМОЙЛОВ

"I bought seven lottery tickets and they all turned out to be winners!"

—КУПИЛ СЕМЬ БИЛЕТОВ, И ВСЕ ОКАЗАЛИСЬ ВЫИГРЫШНЫМИ!

G. Iorsh
Г. ИОРШ

Serenade

СЕРЕНАДА

V. Solov'ev
В. СОЛОВЬЕВ

"Good work, Petrov. You went a whole month without making a single defective part!"
"Yeah, I was on vacation!"

—МОЛОДЕЦ, ПЕТРОВ, ЗА ЦЕЛЫЙ МЕСЯЦ НИ ОДНОЙ БРАКОВАННОЙ ДЕТАЛИ!
—ТАК Я ЖЕ В ОТПУСКЕ БЫЛ!

V. Bokovnia
В. БОКОВНЯ

94

"We usually drive the mammoths into new high-rise apartment projects. There's no way they'll ever get out of those pits."

—МЫ ОБЫЧНО МАМОНТОВ В НОВЫЕ РАЙОНЫ ЗАГОНЯЕМ, ИЗ ЭТИХ ЯМ ИМ УЖЕ НЕ ВЫЛЕЗТИ.

G. Karavaeva

Г. КАРАВАЕВА

95

"Doctor, please give me a prescription for some antigreed pills, and as large a supply as possible!"

—ВЫПИШИТЕ МНЕ ТАБЛЕТОК ОТ ЖАДНОСТИ ДА ПОБОЛЬШЕ, ДОКТОР, ПОБОЛЬШЕ!

V. Dubov
В. ДУБОВ

96

R. Dzhashi
Р. ДЖАШИ

N. Krutikov
Н. КРУТИКОВ

"We'll get him off that bench. Our boom box is more powerful than his!"

—А МЫ ЕГО С ЛАВОЧКИ ВЫЖИВЕМ, У НАС АППАРАТУРА ПОМОЩНЕЙ!

L. Filippova
Л. ФИЛИППОВА

V. Soldatov
В. СОЛДАТОВ

"I've forgotten the music."
"And I've forgotten the words."

A. Pomazkov
А. ПОМАЗКОВ

"Klava, the boss has left for the day. Take all the meat and fish items off the menu . . ."

—КЛАВА, ДИРЕКТОР ПОШЕЛ ДОМОЙ. ВЫЧЕРКНИ ИЗ МЕНЮ ВСЕ МЯСНОЕ И ЗАЛИВНОЕ . . .

E. Shcheglov
Е. ЩЕГЛОВ

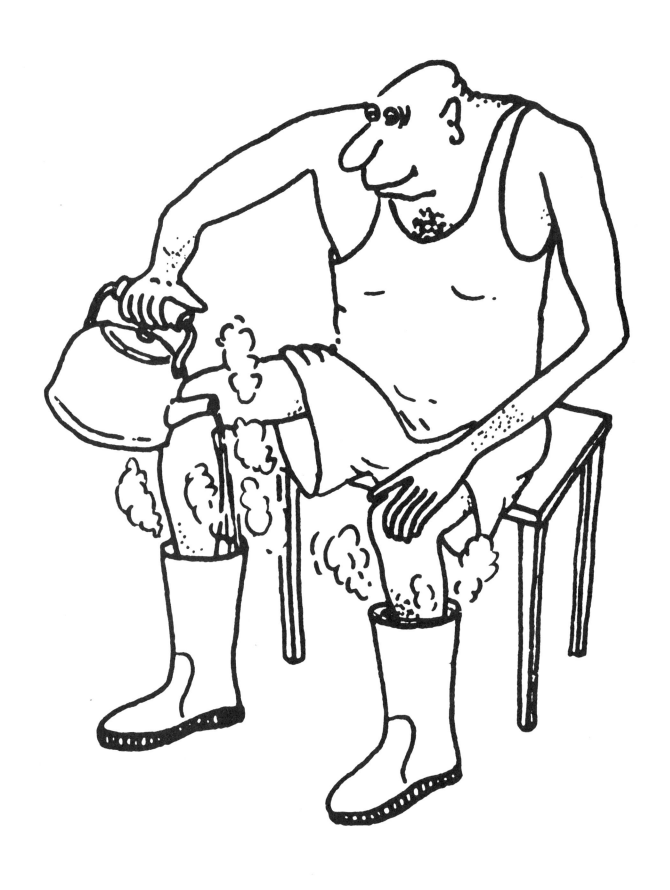

E. Milutka
Е. МИЛУТКА

E. Milutka
Е. МИЛУТКА

104

M. Skobelev
М. СКОБЕЛЕВ

N. Belevtsev
Н. БЕЛЕВЦЕВ

V. Mokhov
В. МОХОВ

N. Belevtsev

Н. БЕЛЕВЦЕВ

M. Vaisbord
М. ВАЙСБОРД

A. Panasenko

А. ПАНАСЕНКО

111

A. Panasenko
А. ПАНАСЕНКО

"We set out to invent the bicycle, but we made some changes and additions during the development phase."

—НАЧИНАЛИ МЫ ИЗОБРЕТАТЬ ВЕЛОСИПЕД, А ПО ХОДУ ДЕЛА В КОНСТРУКЦИЮ ВНОСИЛИСЬ ИЗМЕНЕНИЯ И ДОПОЛНЕНИЯ.

G. Ogorodnikov
Г. ОГОРОДНИКОВ

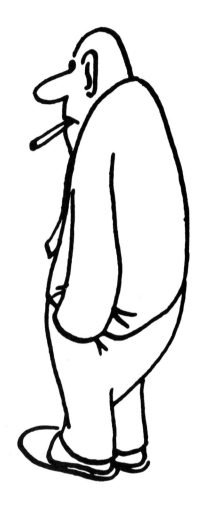

"When I grow up, I'm going to make you play the violin and make Mom drink cod-liver oil."

—ВЫРАСТУ БОЛЬШОЙ, ТЕБЯ ЗАСТАВЛЮ ИГРАТЬ НА СКРИПКЕ, А МАМУ—ПИТЬ РЫБИЙ ЖИР.

V. Spel'nikov
В. СПЕЛЬНИКОВ

"Look, an apple is about to land on him—he's got a great future
ahead of him in physics . . ."

—ПЕРСПЕКТИВНЫЙ ФИЗИК, НА НЕГО ВОТ-ВОТ ЯБЛОКО УПАДЕТ . . .

G. Ogorodnikov
Г. ОГОРОДНИКОВ

"Look over there. Our neighbor has even taken up skiing so that we'll never be out of her sight."

—СМОТРИ, СОСЕДКА ДАЖЕ НА ЛЫЖИ ВСТАЛА, ЧТОБЫ НЕ УПУСТИТЬ НАС ИЗ ВИДА.

S. Spasskii

С. СПАССКИЙ

115

An exhibit called "Art and Sports."

ВЫСТАВКА "ИСКУССТВО И СПОРТ".

Iu. Stepanov
Ю. СТЕПАНОВ

116

Start

I. Novikov
И. НОВИКОВ

V. Shkarban
В. ШКАРБАН

*"Take the little goat off the list of our employees and issue a statement:
'Fired at his own request.'"*

—ВЫЧЕРКНИТЕ КОЗЛИКА ИЗ СПИСКА НАШИХ СОТРУДНИКОВ И ПОДГОТОВЬТЕ ПРИКАЗ:
"УВОЛИТЬ ПО СОБСТВЕННОМУ ЖЕЛАНИЮ."

K. Nevler and M. Ushats

К. НЕВЛЕР И М. УШАЦ

"I see Petrov is not at work again. The first thing I'll do when I get there is hit him with a reprimand."

—ОПЯТЬ ПЕТРОВ ПРОГУЛЯЛ. СЕЙЧАС ПРИДУ НА РАБОТУ—ПЕРВЫМ ДЕЛОМ ВКАЧУ ЕМУ ВЫГОВОР.

S. Spasskii
С. СПАССКИЙ

"I kept telling him not to eat in this cafeteria!"

—ГОВОРИЛА Я ЕМУ: НЕ ЕШЬ В ЭТОЙ СТОЛОВОЙ!

G. Andrianov

Г. АНДРИАНОВ

121

"We'll listen to music, we'll dance!"

N. Belevtsev
Н. БЕЛЕВЦЕВ

The chef: "Well, now, the fish is cooked, but the potatoes aren't quite done yet!"

ШЕФ: —НУ ЧТО Ж, РЫБА УЖЕ ГОТОВА, А КАРТОШКА ЕЩЕ СЫРОВАТА!

I. Novikov
И. НОВИКОВ

"Watch out, she's poisonous!"

—ОСТОРОЖНО, ЯДОВИТАЯ!

A. Aleshichev
А. АЛЕШИЧЕВ

E. Milutka
Е. МИЛУТКА

E. Milutka
Е. МИЛУТКА

R. Drukman
Р. ДРУКМАН

E. Raputova
Э. РАПУТОВА

128

A. Sukharev

А. СУХАРЕВ

E. Milutka

Е. МИЛУТКА

I. Novikov
И. НОВИКОВ

E. Milutka
Е. МИЛУТКА

E. Val'ter
Э. ВАЛЬТЕР

E. Milutka
Е. МИЛУТКА

N. Malov
Н. МАЛОВ

M. Valiakhmetov

М. ВАЛИАХМЕТОВ

Part 3
SOCIAL VICES

"They've found a common language, but now they can't even talk . . ."

—НАШЛИ ОБЩИЙ ЯЗЫК, НО ГОВОРИТЬ УЖЕ НЕ МОГУТ . . .

E. Shukaev

Е. ШУКАЕВ

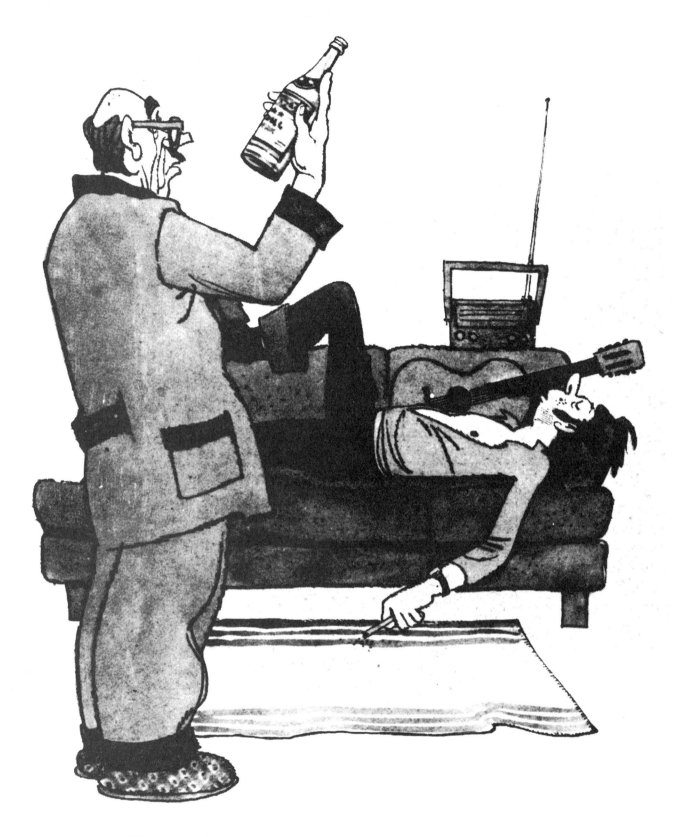

"I've sure raised a selfish kid—he could have left me at least a drop."

—НЕЧЕГО СКАЗАТЬ, ВЫРАСТИЛ ЭГОИСТА—ХОТЬ БЫ КАПЛЮ ОСТАВИЛ.

L. Samoilov
Л. САМОЙЛОВ

138

"Hey, man!"

A. Egorov
А. ЕГОРОВ

Sobriety tests

ПРОВЕРКА НА ТРЕЗВОСТЬ

A. Aleshichev
А. АЛЕШИЧЕВ

A. Aleshichev
А. АЛЕШИЧЕВ

"I have no complaints about my suitors. Some of them loved me to death."

— НА ПОКЛОННИКОВ Я НЕ ЖАЛУЮСЬ, ИНЫЕ МЕНЯ ДО СМЕРТИ ЛЮБИЛИ.

L. Samoilov
Л. САМОЙЛОВ

142

A. Pshenianikov
А. ПШЕНЯНИКОВ

"I warned you that you'd never be able to eat this without vodka."

—Я ЖЕ ВАС ПРЕДУПРЕЖДАЛА—БЕЗ ВОДКИ ЭТО ЕСТЬ НЕВОЗМОЖНО.

V. Bokovnia
В. БОКОВНЯ

"No matter when I turn on the TV, they're always showing 'Animal World.'"

—КОГДА НЕ ВКЛЮЧУ, ВСЕ ВРЕМЯ "В МИРЕ ЖИВОТНЫХ".

145

S. Spasskii
С. СПАССКИЙ

S. Tiunin
С. ТЮНИН

146

"Come on, Simon, no hard feelings. We decided to hold a wake for you in advance because that's the only excuse we could think of . . ."

—ТЫ ЭТО . . . СЕМЕН, НЕ ОБИЖАЙСЯ, МЫ ТВОИ ПОМИНКИ РЕШИЛИ АВАНСОМ СПРАВИТЬ, А ТО ПОВОДА НЕТ . . .

V. Mochalov
В. МОЧАЛОВ

L. Storozhuk
Л. СТОРОЖУК

148

Part 4
POLITICS AND BUREAUCRACY

G. Basyrov
Г. БАСЫРОВ

E. Osipov
Е. ОСИПОВ

E. Milutka
Е. МИЛУТКА

Perpetual motion machine

ПЕРПЕТУУМ

S. Tiunin
С. ТЮНИН

152

I. Novikov
И. НОВИКОВ

O. Estis
О. ЭСТИС

I. Smirnov
И. СМИРНОВ

L. Levitskii
Л. ЛЕВИЦКИЙ

156

"We made this gown from leftover material!"

—ЭТО ПЛАТЬЕ МЫ СШИЛИ ИЗ СЭКОНОМЛЕННОГО МАТЕРИАЛА!

E. Shabel'nik
Е. ШАБЕЛЬНИК

V. Dmitriuk

В. ДМИТРЮК

158

159

I. Smirnov
И. СМИРНОВ

"Just think, when they assigned that emperor to our department
he wasn't wearing any clothes . . ."

—ПОДУМАТЬ ТОЛЬКО, КОГДА ЭТОГО КОРОЛЯ НАЗНАЧИЛИ В НАШУ КОНТОРУ, ОН БЫЛ
СОВЕРШЕННО ГОЛЫЙ . . .

L. Filippova
Л. ФИЛИППОВА

160

I. Smirnov
И. СМИРНОВ

S. Tiunin
С. ТЮНИН

162

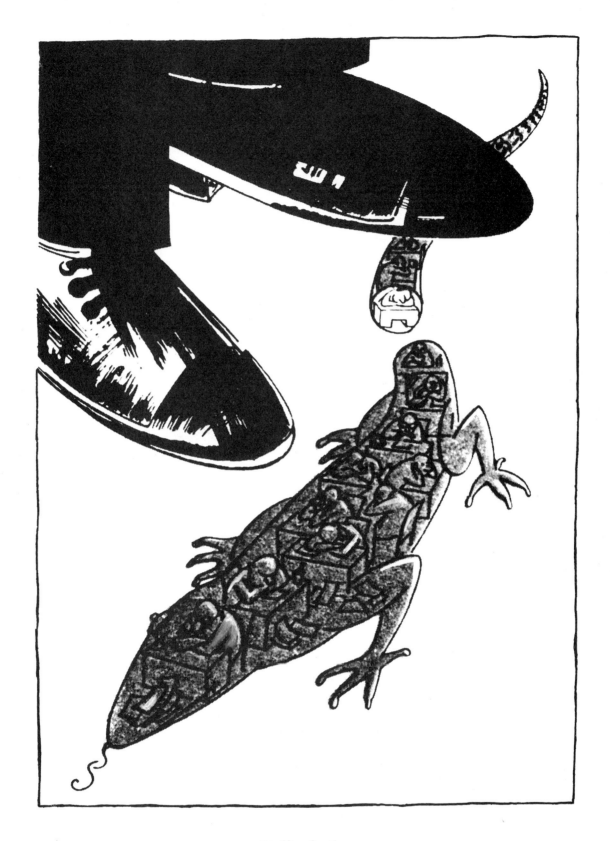

Staff reduction.

СОКРАЩЕНИЕ ШТАТОВ.

163

V. Mokhov

В. МОХОВ

"What's the password?"
"Glasnost."
"Come in."

—ПАРОЛЬ?
—ГЛАСНОСТЬ.
—ПРОХОДИ.

V. Til'man
В. ТИЛЬМАН

164

"Congratulations! Your invention is already being used.
We bought it from a foreign company."

—ПОЗДРАВЛЯЮ! ВАШЕ ИЗОБРЕТЕНИЕ ВНЕДРЕНО. МЫ ЕГО УЖЕ ЗАКУПИЛИ У
ИНОСТРАННОЙ ФИРМЫ.

G. Ogorodnikov

Г. ОГОРОДНИКОВ

"What's this? You have your own opinion?"

—А У ВАС ЧТО, СВОЕ МНЕНИЕ?

E. Vedernikov
Е. ВЕДЕРНИКОВ

"There you are! Now you can fly!"

V. Dmitriuk
В. ДМИТРЮК

I. Smirnov
И. СМИРНОВ

S. Tiunin
С. ТЮНИН

S. Tiunin
С. ТЮНИН

"You're getting sidetracked again!"

E. Osipov

Е. ОСИПОВ

"Grandpa, they're finally using your invention."

—ИЗОБРЕТЕНИЕ ТВОЕ, ДЕДУШКА, ВНЕДРИЛИ.

V. Til'man
В. ТИЛЬМАН

V. Peskov
В. ПЕСКОВ

V. Dmitriuk

В. ДМИТРЮК

174

"This bridge passes inspection."

—СЧИТАТЬ ОБЪЕКТ ПРИНЯТЫМ.

175

E. Shcheglov
Е. ЩЕГЛОВ

G. Magomaev
Г. МАГОМАЕВ

Part 5
ENVIRONMENT

G. Karavaeva
Г. КАРАВАЕВА

"Goodness gracious! What a paradise! We should definitely build a cellulose plant right here."

V. Dmitriuk
В. ДМИТРЮК

178

G. Magomaev
Г. МАГОМАЕВ

Voices from the forest.

ГОЛОСА ЛЕСА.

G. Karavaeva
Г. КАРАВАЕВА

V. Shkarban
В. ШКАРБАН

N. Malov

Н. МАЛОВ

"Let's spend the winter here, on this heating pipe . . ."

—А ЗИМОВАТЬ БУДЕМ ЗДЕСЬ, НА ТЕПЛОТРАССЕ . . .

E. Vedernikov
Е. ВЕДЕРНИКОВ

"Look, that's just how the swan died in our pond by the chemical plant."

—СМОТРИ, ТОЧНО ТАК ЖЕ УМИРАЛ ЛЕБЕДЬ НА НАШЕМ ПРУДУ ВОЗЛЕ ХИМЗАВОДА.

E. Shukaev
Е. ШУКАЕВ

184

V. Dmitriuk

В. ДМИТРЮК

"Now let's make ourselves a clean table!"

—СЕЙЧАС ОРГАНИЗУЕМ ЧИСТЫЙ СТОЛИК!

E. Shabel'nik
Е. ШАБЕЛЬНИК

"I didn't know that snow is actually white!"

—А СНЕГ-ТО, ОКАЗЫВАЕТСЯ, БЕЛЫЙ!

E. Gurov
Е. ГУРОВ

"To be or not to be?"

—БЫТЬ ИЛИ НЕ БЫТЬ?

E. Gavrilin
Е. ГАВРИЛИН

"Wow! Your father must be a famous big-game hunter!"
"No, he's the head of a wildlife preserve."

—УХ ТЫ! ТВОЙ ОТЕЦ, НАВЕРНО, ЗНАМЕНИТЫЙ ОХОТНИК?
—НЕТ, ОН ДИРЕКТОР ЗАПОВЕДНИКА.

L. Samoilov

Л. САМОЙЛОВ

"On your left is a functioning church that has no architectural value. And on your right, comrades, is a monument protected by the State."

—СЛЕВА—ДЕЙСТВУЮЩАЯ ЦЕРКОВЬ, НЕ ИМЕЮЩАЯ АРХИТЕКТУРНОЙ ЦЕННОСТИ, А СПРАВА, ТОВАРИЩИ, ПАМЯТНИК АРХИТЕКТУРЫ, ОХРАНЯЕМЫЙ ГОСУДАРСТВОМ.

V. Skrylev
В. СКРЫЛЕВ

"I only cut it down to put it out of its misery . . ."

—СРУБИЛ ТОЛЬКО ЗАТЕМ, ЧТОБЫ НЕ МУЧИЛАСЬ . . .

V. Shkarban
В. ШКАРБАН

N. Malov

Н. МАЛОВ